Charles Darwin

Ann Fullick

Heinemann Library
Chicago, Illinois

© 2001 Reed Educational & Professional Publishing
Published by Heinemann Library,
an imprint of Reed Educational & Professional Publishing,
100 N. LaSalle, Suite 1010
Chicago, IL 60602
Customer Service 888-454-2279
Visit our website at www.heinemannlibrary.com

Designed by AMR
Illustrated by Art Construction and Nina O'Connell
Originated by Ambassador Litho
Printed in Hong Kong

05 04 03 02 01
10 9 8 7 6 5 4 3 2 1

Library of Congress Cataloging-in-Publication Data
Fullick, Ann, 1956-
    Charles Darwin / Ann Fullick.
      p. cm. – (Groundbreakers)
    Includes bibliographical references (p.) and index.
    Summary: A biography of the English naturalist who, after collecting plants and
animals from around the world, came up with the theory of evolution by natural selection.
    ISBN 1-57572-368-9
    1. Darwin, Charles, 1809-1882—Juvenile literature. 2.
Naturalists—England—Biography—Juvenile literature. [1. Darwin, Charles, 1809-1882. 2.
Naturalists.] I. Title. II. Series.

QH31.D2 F86 2000
576.8'092—dc21
[B]   00-025093

Acknowledgments
The Publishers would like to thank the following for permission to reproduce photographs:
Mary Evans, pp. 4, 5, 12, 20, 23, 31, 33, 36; The Bridgeman Art Library, p. 6; Hulton Getty, pp.
7, 8, 10, 11, 24, 28, 37; NHPA, pp. 9, 17, 25; Oxford Scientific Films, pp. 13, 15, 16, 29, 40;
Bruce Coleman, pp. 19, 35, 39, 41, 43; English Heritage Photo Library, pp. 21, 22, 30, 42; Katz
Pictures, p. 32; Ardea, p. 34; Corbis/Bettmann, p. 38.

Cover photograph reproduced with permission of English Heritage Photo Library.

Some words are shown in bold, **like this.** You can find out what
they mean by looking in the glossary.

Contents

Changing Times

The early years of the nineteenth century saw the birth of a man whose theories would change forever the way people looked at the world arount them. His name was Charles Darwin.

Intolerant times

England in those days was not a tolerant society. Many people still believed that every word of the Bible was absolutely true. Life was governed by a very strict moral code. Some people behaved in ways that broke the code—but never in public. As the century progressed, and Queen Victoria came to the throne, the British Empire stretched around the globe, and the British people were proud of their position in the world. Victorian capitalism saw the birth and success of many major industries. The rich were rich, the poor were poor, and everyone knew his or her place and station in life.

In a wealthy home such as the one Charles Darwin was born into, people wore fine clothes, ate well, and had servants to take care of the household chores. Families were large. This family is gathered together in the evening to listen to the father telling a story.

A new world view

It was in these strict and moral times that Charles Darwin grew up, but he was fortunate enough to be born into a family of thinkers—men and women of ideas. By the time Darwin published his groundbreaking idea—that living things had not been created as they are now all at once by God, but had **evolved** over millions of years—society itself had changed.

Although Darwin's ideas were met with fury and opposition in some places, many people were ready to listen to and understand what he had to say. His vision has changed the face of science forever, and much of our modern understanding of **ecology, genetics,** evolution, and conservation stems from the work of Charles Darwin, perhaps the most amazing Victorian of them all.

Charles Robert Darwin was born in 1809 and died in 1882. In his life, he went from being an academic failure to becoming one of the greatest biologists the world has ever known.

The Darwin Family

Charles Darwin was born in Shrewsbury, England, into a family of well-known intellectuals. They were people of strong views who were not afraid to express them.

His grandfather, Erasmus Darwin, was a doctor who was also internationally known for his poetic descriptions of the natural world, published in his book *Zoonomia*. Erasmus saw **reproduction** as the key to understanding the workings of nature, as his grandson would years later. He was a member of the **Lunar Society,** which included a number of famous men such as James Watt, Joseph Priestley, and Josiah Wedgwood, all of whom had played an important part in the **Industrial Revolution.** They met to discuss the role of science and invention in a changing society.

AM I NOT A MAN & A BROTHER

Erasmus's son, Robert Waring Darwin, was also a doctor, and a very good one. He was both successful and wealthy, because he combined medicine with a business career. He made a fortune that provided his children with an independent income for the rest of their lives.

*This painting has an antislavery message. Both of Darwin's grandfathers were free thinkers who supported the **abolition** of slavery, freedom of enterprise, and freedom of expression. Slavery was finally abolished in the British Empire in 1833.*

Charles was the fifth of six children and his parents' second son. This picture shows Charles at age seven, with his younger sister, Catherine.

The birth of Charles

Robert Darwin married Susannah Wedgwood, daughter of his father's friend Josiah, who founded the famous Wedgwood china business. She was much more conventional in her thinking than her husband, and was devoted to her Christian faith. Charles Robert Darwin was born on February 12, 1809, in Shrewsbury, in the west of England.

Charles's early childhood seems to have been happy and uneventful, but when he was only eight years old, his mother died. His older sisters Marianne, Caroline, and Susan took over his care. They were devoted to their little brother and shared with him the strong religious beliefs that they learned from their mother. Thus, in spite of the loss he suffered, Charles grew up in a warm and comfortable family, loved and secure, exposed to both **radical,** intellectual discussion and to traditional values. The importance of these varied influences can be seen throughout his life, in the ideas he had and in the man he became.

In Darwin's words:

Robert Darwin was rich, and he enjoyed a comfortable way of life and the best of food. Charles later recalled that his father became *"very corpulent [fat], so that he was the largest man whom I ever saw."* This is probably not the way any of us would wish to be remembered!

7

The Young Man

Charles Darwin started his school career by attending a small local school. However, like many children before and after him, he did not really enjoy school, and it was not until he was much older that he began to take real pleasure in learning and finding out new things.

Like all young men in his social position, Charles was sent to boarding school at the age of nine—but only as far as the local **public school,** Shrewsbury, where his brother was a student. He coped with living away from his family and was close enough for frequent visits home. However, Shrewsbury was run very strictly, with only traditional subjects, and Charles did not like it at all.

Charles was much happier when he could spend time with some friends. He also became very interested in collecting minerals and bird-watching, and he developed a passion for chemistry that he shared with his older brother, Erasmus. However, Charles's time at school was not really a success, and at the tender age of sixteen, he was sent to Edinburgh University in Scotland, to follow in the family tradition and study medicine.

In Darwin's words:

Charles Darwin later made the kind of confession that a school like Shrewsbury would not want to hear from such a famous former student: *"The school as a means of education to me was simply a blank."*

Shrewsbury School was where Charles Darwin studied, rather unsuccessfully, until the age of sixteen.

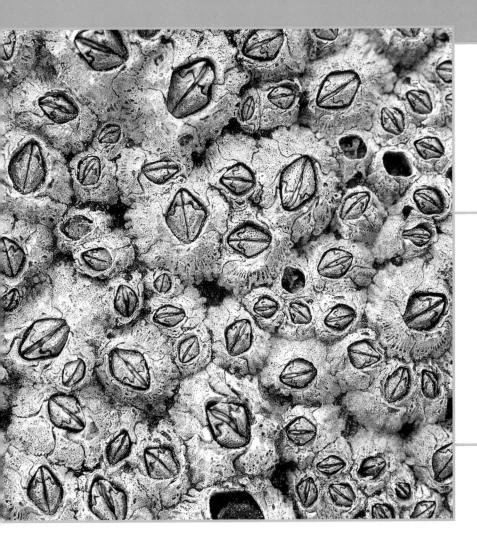

*It was marine **invertebrates** like these barnacles, living in massive colonies of individuals, that first fascinated Charles Darwin during his student days in Edinburgh.*

The struggling student

Charles was not much happier with his Edinburgh education than he had been at Shrewsbury. He enjoyed his chemistry classes, but found geology "incredibly dull!"

As part of his studies, Charles had to watch doctors perform surgery. When these experiences made him feel sick, he decided that perhaps medicine was not for him. However, his time at Edinburgh was not all bad. It was there that he started to become an active **naturalist,** collecting and minutely examining **marine** organisms. It was this hobby which later became the driving force of his whole career.

In Darwin's words:

After Robert Jameson's lectures on geology (a subject Darwin would later learn to love), Darwin wrote: *"The sole effect they produced on me was the determination never as long as I lived to read a book on Geology, or in any way to study the science."*

Cambridge Days

Once Charles had decided he was not cut out to be a doctor, his father suggested that he become a clergyman, or minister. The first step to taking holy orders was to get a degree at one of the English universities, so Charles enrolled at Cambridge University.

A reluctant student

Even at Cambridge, Charles found studying hard work. He disliked mathematics and was bad at it. By working hard in **classics** and **divinity,** he managed to pass his final exams, but earned only an ordinary degree, not an honors degree! He spent much of his time hunting with friends, and even took an interest in music, although he had a poor sense of tone and rhythm. He did, however, become an dedicated **naturalist** and built up quite a collection of insects.

While at Cambridge, Charles also made one of the most influential friendships of his life—with John Henslow, a professor of **botany.** He attended his lectures, accompanied him on field trips, and became a family friend. He learned enormous amounts about the scientific study of natural history and developed skills which would help him greatly in the future. He read constantly and developed a great desire to travel as widely as possible so he could continue his studies as a naturalist. His chance would soon come.

*After a few months of intense studying in the classics—which he had avoided before—Charles Darwin was accepted to Christ's College at Cambridge University, where he studied to become a **vicar.***

After earning his degree, Charles stayed in Cambridge for a short time, continuing his studies with Professor Henslow, and finally becoming excited about the study of geology, which now fascinated him. He felt more and more that a life serving the Church was not for him. He did not want to become a vicar—but what other future could he find?

The die is cast

In August 1831, Henslow was informed that Captain Robert FitzRoy was looking for a naturalist who would be his companion on his next voyage. On FitzRoy's previous voyage, the ship's captain had had a nervous breakdown, probably caused by the loneliness of his command position on the long voyage. At the time, a captain was not allowed to associate with crew members. FitzRoy, who was second in command, had been forced to take over. Now that he was a captain, he was determined not to suffer the same fate. He planned to take someone to be his companion rather than just a crew member. When Henslow was asked to suggest a naturalist for the journey, he knew the very man—Charles Robert Darwin.

Robert FitzRoy, captain of the H.M.S. Beagle, *was the man who would open the door to a whole new world for Charles Darwin.*

11

Darwin the Adventurer

When H.M.S. *Beagle* set sail on December 27, 1831, 22-year-old Charles Darwin was aboard as the captain's **naturalist** and companion. He had first had to overcome the opposition of both his father—who worried about his career—and Captain FitzRoy himself, who felt that the shape of Darwin's nose suggested he did not have the character needed for such a voyage!

A new world

You CAN FOLLOW THE *BEAGLE*'S VOYAGE ON THE MAP ON PAGE 18.

The *Beagle* set off to chart the coast of South America and the South Sea Islands. Charles planned to study mainly geology on his voyage, and to a large extent this is what he did. Yet it was some of the work he regarded as less important at the time that would have the strongest impact on his thinking later. At the start of the trip, Charles felt that he was a poorly trained amateur, but as the five-year voyage progressed, his confidence in his abilities grew. He suffered badly from seasickness on the first part of the journey, and was greatly relieved when they finally reached Bahia (now Salvador), Brazil, in February 1832.

The H.M.S. Beagle *was the ship that carried Charles Darwin on the voyage of a lifetime.*

Eating the evidence!

In July 1832, the *Beagle* moved to Montevideo to spend two years charting the waters around South America. Charles spent much time exploring the **pampas.** He loved the open-air life, and collected many interesting plant and animal specimens, but he almost did not make his most important South American discovery. He was familiar with the common **rhea** (an ostrichlike bird) of the area, and had heard talk of a different form found in the south. The party had cooked and eaten one of this new type of rhea before Darwin realized what he was doing! He sent the remains of the meal back to England to be identified as a new **species**, later named *Rhea darwinii* in his honor.

The richness of the Brazilian rain forests astonished and delighted Charles Darwin.

In Darwin's words:

The *Beagle* spent April, May, and June around Rio de Janeiro, and Darwin's journal records his reactions to this amazing new country and its population:

"The day has passed delightfully. Delight itself, however, is a weak term to express the feelings of a naturalist who, for the first time, has wandered by himself in a Brazilian forest. The elegance of the grasses, the novelty of the parasitic plants, the beauty of the flowers, the glossy green of the vegetation, but above all the general luxuriance of the vegetation, filled me with admiration."

The Galápagos Islands

As the *Beagle* continued her voyage around Tierra del Fuego and the Falkland Islands, off the southern coast of South America, Darwin regularly sent specimens of the animals, plants, and fossils he was discovering back to Henslow in England. However, he heard nothing in return and became very concerned that the material he was collecting was simply not good enough. Henslow was actually delighted and had written Darwin several letters, but they did not reach the *Beagle* until July 1834. This approval meant a lot to Darwin and renewed his enthusiasm for collecting specimens. Now, the voyage continued toward the Galápagos **archipelago.**

YOU CAN FOLLOW THE *BEAGLE*'S VOYAGE ON THE MAP ON PAGE 18.

Darwin discovered a number of new fossils during his exploration of South America. The ways in which they resembled and differed from modern **species** *influenced his thinking in years to come. This is an artist's impression of* Megatherium, *a giant land sloth whose fossils Darwin discovered in South America. It was as big as an elephant.*

In Darwin's words:

In spite of his fascination for the Galápagos Islands and their inhabitants, Darwin did not recognize the implications of the differences he had seen between the **populations** living on different islands, as he later recorded in his journal:

"My attention was drawn to this fact by the Vice-Governor, Mr. Lawson, declaring that the tortoises differed from different islands, and that he could with certainty tell from which island any one was brought. I did not for some time pay sufficient attention to this statement, and I have already partially mingled together the collections from two of the islands. I never dreamed that islands, about fifty or sixty miles apart, and most of them in sight of each other, formed of precisely the same rocks, placed under a quite similar climate, would have been differently tenanted."

Galápagos!

The Galápagos Islands are volcanic, with lots of
bare black rock and stunted trees and plants.
Darwin had the opportunity to land and make
observations on a number of the islands, and he
found them fascinating. He was very interested in
the giant tortoises that roamed the islands,
following them and trying to pick them up,
though he did not think to actually collect one to
bring home. Darwin also found the birds amazing, partly because
they were so tame. On each island, he would collect all the birds
he needed, killing them simply with a stick, since they made no
attempt to fly away! He was particularly interested in the
different finches and mockingbirds he found on each island.

*The giant tortoises of the
Galápagos Islands amazed
Charles Darwin. The tortoise
population on each island is
quite distinct in appearance
from the tortoises on any
other island in the area.*

The Iguana Enigma

As Darwin found, the animals and plants of the Galápagos **archipelago** are incredibly varied. The iguanas in particular made a great impression on him, because the observations he made of them reminded him strongly of the notes he had made when observing **rheas** in South America.

You can follow the *Beagle*'s voyage on the map on page 18.

In most places where they are found, iguanas are land-living reptiles that enjoy hot, dry conditions. Just as he had anticipated, Darwin found a **species** of iguana living inland on the dry part of the Galápagos Islands. To his amazement, though, he also found a different species that not only lived on the shores of the islands, but went into the water to eat the seaweed found on the rocks, among the crashing waves.

Reptiles are *poikilothermal*, meaning cold-blooded, and they need to keep warm to be able to move. The **marine** iguanas have had to adapt to survive in the water long enough to feed. They grow very large, and as they sunbathe on the rocks, their skin turns black. This means they can absorb and store as much energy from the sun as possible. When they have raised their body temperatures enough, they enter the water to feed, coming out again only when their body temperature drops too low for them to function properly.

The discovery of these amazing marine iguanas on the Galápagos Islands, as well as the inland iguana species, gave the young Charles Darwin plenty to think about.

As the *Beagle* visited the many islands of the Galápagos archipelago, Darwin made detailed notes, observations, and drawings, and he sent his shipmates out to make observations, too. Then all of his carefully collected data was taken back on board the ship, to be studied as the voyage continued.

*The Solomon Islands, which lie about 1,000 miles (1,600 kilometers) northeast of Australia, are home to many unique species. For example, on three of the islands, the coconut palms are **pollinated** by a rare type of bat called a flying fox, which is threatened with extinction. If one species disappears, others will be affected, so protecting them is vital.*

Because islands are isolated, their animals and plants are often unique. Just as Darwin did, scientists today like to study these island communities to help them understand **evolution.** Islands, however, are also particularly vulnerable to the damage people can cause by cutting down trees, introducing industries, testing weapons, or through heavy tourism. Seventy-five percent of the animals that have most recently become extinct have been island species, so some scientists suggest that we should concentrate our conservation efforts on saving these areas, which are very small, but very rich in different forms of life that are found in few other places.

The End of the Journey

The Galápagos Islands were the last major stopping point for the *Beagle*. When Captain Robert FitzRoy steered his ship away from the volcanic **archipelago,** he set sail for home, by a route that took the ship right round the world.

The five-year voyage of the *Beagle* provided Darwin with plenty of time for reading and reflection on all he had observed. His work on geology really excited him, and he became convinced that Charles Lyell's geological ideas were correct. He wrote about many of his findings on the voyage and had his letters read to the **Geological Society,** of which Lyell was president. More importantly, Darwin began to reflect on the relevance of the living organisms—the animals and plants—that he had seen, drawn, and collected. As he thought about what he had observed, he began to realize that his findings might be considerably more important than just a group of newly discovered **species.**

This map of the Beagle's *voyage shows the journey that introduced Charles Darwin to some of the vast variety of life around the world and gave him the ideas on which he based his life's work.*

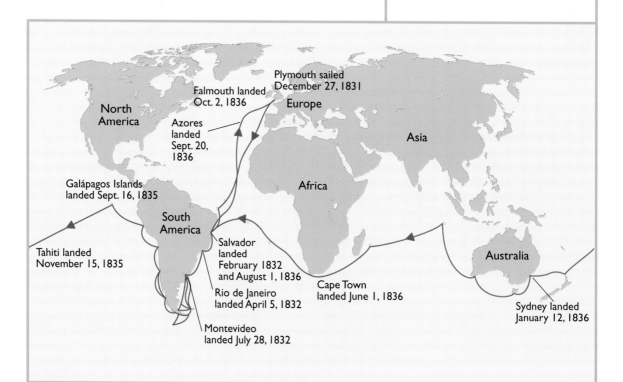

Plymouth sailed December 27, 1831

Falmouth landed Oct. 2, 1836

Europe

North America

Azores landed Sept. 20, 1836

Asia

Galápagos Islands landed Sept. 16, 1835

Africa

South America

Tahiti landed November 15, 1835

Salvador landed February 1832 and August 1, 1836

Australia

Cape Town landed June 1, 1836

Rio de Janeiro landed April 5, 1832

Sydney landed January 12, 1836

Montevideo landed July 28, 1832

Home!

Robert FitzRoy survived his first voyage as captain without having a breakdown, thanks in part to the companionship of Charles Darwin. They had had two major quarrels along the way, about slavery and their political beliefs, but most of the time, they had given each other mutual support and understanding.

On October 2, 1836, H.M.S. *Beagle* slipped quietly back into Falmouth harbor at the end of her epic voyage. No one imagined then that the journey would be remembered for many years because of the work Darwin had carried out as the *Beagle* charted the New World. Charles rushed off to visit his family back in Shrewsbury, where he enjoyed a happy break before returning to supervise the removal of his specimens and notebooks from the *Beagle*. He was ready for the real work to begin.

Charles Lyell (1797–1875) was born in Scotland and studied law as a young man. However, he soon decided that he wanted to be a geologist, and in time he became professor of geology at the University of London. He produced a massive three-volume book, *Principles of Geology,* which challenged the idea that the appearance of the earth was the result of events which all happened at the same time—a belief called *catastrophism.* Lyell's theory was that the appearance of the earth was the result of ongoing processes, such as rivers, volcanoes, and the movement of sedimentary rocks, constantly changing the earth's surface. Much to Lyell's surprise, his ideas were widely accepted. They certainly influenced Charles Darwin—and much later, when Darwin published his theories of **evolution,** Lyell returned Darwin's support.

Once back in England, Darwin had to find homes for all his specimens, which ranged from mammals and birds—like this Galápagos mockingbird—to large lumps of rock. Most of the specimens were preserved in alcohol, and many of them still exist today.

After the Beagle

For the first few months after his return, Darwin worked in Cambridge. He had all his specimens sent there. He tried to persuade other people to look at the animals and plants he had collected, so he would be free to work on his geological ideas. Between 1838 and 1842, various illustrated books were published about the birds, mammals, reptiles, fossils, and fish he had collected. By that time, Darwin had left Cambridge—although he loved the town—to become part of the thriving community of top scientists who lived and worked in London.

Geological tales

The years 1837–39 were full ones for Darwin, as he busied himself with the vast amounts of geological material from his voyage. He sorted the specimens and began work on a number of books—about coral reefs, South America, and volcanic islands. He enjoyed both his membership in the **Geological Society** and working with his hero, Charles Lyell. In 1839, he was made a Fellow of the **Royal Society** in recognition of his work.

John Gould, an ornithologist, shared his insight into the Galápagos finches with Darwin and helped him develop his theories.

JOHN GOULD

John Gould (1804–1881) was a fairly well-known **ornithologist** who worked on the birds Darwin brought back from the Galápagos Islands. Gould focused closely on the finches, recognizing thirteen **species** that he divided into four separate groups. He made it very clear to Darwin that these finches were quite distinct but closely related species—adding fuel to the fires of Darwin's thinking.

Personal thoughts

Charles was becoming increasingly involved in his work, but he was also becoming very aware of the limitations of a life that held nothing but that work. In April 1838, he scribbled a note to himself on the back of a letter suggesting the possibility of marriage, and in July, he drew up a list of the pros and cons of marrying his cousin Emma. The disadvantages included loss of freedom and less time for scientific work, but there were many advantages as well.

In Darwin's words:

"My God, it is intolerable to think of spending one's whole life, like a neuter bee, working, working, & nothing after all...No, no won't do...Imagine living all one's day solitarily in smoky dirty London House...Only picture to yourself a nice soft wife on a sofa with good fire, & books & music perhaps... Compare this vision with the dingy reality of Grt. Marlbro' St.

Marry...Mary [spelling mistake!]*... Marry QED."*

Once he had made the decision to marry, Charles did not delay. In November 1838, he proposed to his cousin, Emma Wedgwood, and she accepted him. They were married on January 29, 1839, and set up a home together at 12 Upper Gower Street in London.

The Family Man

When Charles Darwin married his cousin Emma, he gained a life partner who would support him and act as his friend and confidante for many years. Although Charles made the decision to marry in a rather cold-blooded way, there is no doubt that he and Emma shared a remarkably close and loving relationship.

Within a year of their marriage, Charles and Emma were delighted with the birth of their first child, a son named William Erasmus. However, in the early years of William's life, Darwin's own health began to deteriorate. He had always had a few problems, but now he suffered increasing stomach pain, heart palpitations, and headaches.

As Darwin began to develop his ideas of **natural selection,** his symptoms worsened. He was all too aware of the problems his ideas were going to create when they were revealed to society. It seems likely that this anxiety was the main cause of his symptoms.

At the age of 31, Charles Darwin was a successful geologist and scientist with a wife and small family, but his health was already deteriorating.

By 1842, the Darwin family decided to leave the pressures of London and move with their son, William, and daughter, Anne, to Down House, in the village of Downe, Kent. It was a beautiful house in a beautiful setting, but things did not start well. A few days after they moved in, Emma gave birth to a daughter, Mary Eleanor, but the baby died within three weeks. In spite of this tragedy, the family grew to love the house and spent many happy and successful years there.

Down House was a home that Darwin and his family loved. This was where he and Emma lived with their large brood of children, and where he worked for years on his ideas of natural selection.

Emma's contribution

Emma's support was vital to Charles, and she gave it willingly, even though they had very different ideas. She was a deeply religious woman, and for some time, Charles did not tell her his thoughts on natural selection because he thought they might cause tensions. Eventually, he told her where his work was leading him. It caused Emma great distress to think that her husband was moving away—as she saw it—from a belief in a creator God. Fortunately, their love was so strong that they remained close in spite of these differences, and Emma continued to act as a sounding board and confidante for her brilliant husband. This remarkable woman helped make his work possible, while also giving birth to ten children and taking care of those that survived.

Pigeons, Barnacles, and Brainstorming

The Darwin family settled down to life at Down House. The daily routine of the household was arranged to make sure that Charles could complete as much work as possible without taxing his delicate health too much.

A day in the life of Darwin

Charles Darwin got up early every morning to enjoy a short walk and breakfast before working from 8:00 to 9:30 A.M. He read letters until 10:30 A.M., and then worked again until noon. Charles then took another walk around the garden on a path he called the Sandwalk, and would join his children as they played before lunch. After the meal, he read the newspaper to keep up with politics, then spent time answering letters. Emma often read novels to him while he took an afternoon rest; then he had another walk and a final hour's work before dinner.

Charles never sat and chatted after the meal, because he found that stimulating conversation in the evening made him feel ill the next day, which meant he could not work at all! He spent the evenings playing games such as backgammon with Emma, listening to her play the piano, and reading scientific books before going to bed, although he rarely slept well. In spite of his physical weaknesses, Darwin was a driven man.

This was Charles Darwin's study at Down House. Emma made sure that Charles had everything he needed to enable him to concentrate on his work.

The quest

In the years that followed, Darwin developed his ideas on the **evolution** of **species.** He used his findings from the voyage of the *Beagle,* but he also did endless breeding experiments with pigeons, worked with plants, and studied barnacles in minute detail to support his theories of selection.

In Darwin's words:

In November 1839, Darwin wrote to John Henslow: *"I keep on steadily collecting every sort of fact, which may throw light on the origin and variation of species."*

ONGOING IMPACT   Genetic engineering

Darwin used evidence from **selective breeding** experiments to support his ideas of **natural selection.** Today, though, we no longer have to rely on selecting the features we want slowly through a breeding program.
Genetic engineering means it is possible for scientists simply to insert desirable genes into an animal or plant, changing its shape, flavor, or resistance to disease in one single operation. The effect this will have on natural selection and evolution has yet to be seen, and the technique remains controversial.

Darwin selectively bred fancy pigeons, keeping careful records to show the way the birds' characteristics changed when he selected for different features.

Organizing the Evidence

Moving to Down House gave Darwin exactly what he needed: peace, security, and time to work. But he certainly was not isolated, because he had an amazing group of friends, fellow scientists, and breeders, known as the "Down House network." They helped him to gather together the body of evidence he needed to support his theory. They were also trusted colleagues to whom he could gradually expose his developing ideas.

Pulling threads together

Once Darwin had formulated his ideas of **natural selection,** he spent many years trying to put his evidence together in a way that was utterly convincing. He used the results of his breeding experiments, his work on barnacles, and any other material provided for him by members of the Down House network.

While he was working, his children wandered in and out of his study, using his microscopes and "investigating" his experiments. Charles was way ahead of his time in his approach to his children—he encouraged their interest and delighted in their company. Many Victorian fathers did not have very much to do with their children, and believed in the idea that "children should be seen and not heard."

*These heads of Galápagos finches—now known as Darwin's finches—represent a number of different **species** with one common ancestor. They seem to have developed traits to exploit the different feeding opportunities on the islands.*

Surviving dark times

As Darwin struggled to weave his ideas into one all-embracing theory, tragedy hit the family again. In 1851, Charles and Emma lost their oldest daughter, Anne. She died when she was only ten years old, and Darwin's grief is clear in the words of his journal. It took all his resolve to settle back into work—but life with his seven remaining children had to go on.

In Darwin's words:

"Poor dear little Annie …Thank God she hardly suffered at all, and expired as tranquilly as a little angel. Our only consolation is that she passed a short, though joyous life. She was my favourite child."

THOMAS MALTHUS

Malthus (1766–1834) was an English **economist** who studied the growth of **populations.** In the late eighteenth and early nineteenth centuries, he wrote several essays showing that populations **reproduce** at a faster rate than food supplies increase. Malthus predicted that growing populations are controlled, or kept from getting too large, by famine, disease, and war. Malthus's ideas helped Darwin to recognize the main pressure driving selection: in almost all species, more new individuals were produced than could survive in the environment available to that species. Therefore, some had to change and adapt in new ways.

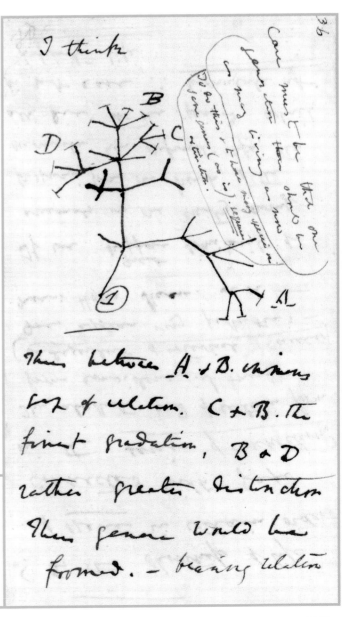

*As Darwin studied his specimens, he began to build up a branching picture of **evolution,** which he tried out in different forms in his notebooks.*

The Other Runner

During the 1840s and 1850s, Darwin continued with his great work. But by 1856, Charles Lyell and other friends were trying to persuade him to publish. They were convinced that the time for his ideas was ripe, and that if he did not go public, someone else would. So Darwin began writing a massive book setting out his theories and evidence. Imagine his reaction when he realized in 1858 that someone else had a good chance to get there first!

Alfred Russel Wallace

Alfred Wallace started work as a land surveyor and then became a teacher. In 1848, he set off on a collecting expedition to South America with Henry Bates, a wealthy amateur insect collector, who had encouraged his interest in natural history. When Wallace returned, his whole collection was destroyed by fire—so he went on another trip with the insurance money!

Wallace had the idea that if a **species** existed in various forms, those that were poorly adapted to any change were likely to die out, leaving only the better-adapted form to survive and breed. Wallace wrote a quick summary of his theory and sent it to the one man he knew whom he thought would be really interested and help him get things published— Charles Darwin.

*Alfred Russel Wallace came from a poor family, with few of Darwin's advantages, but he was a gifted and adventurous **naturalist**. He almost beat Darwin in announcing his ideas on **evolution**.*

Panic sets in

When Darwin received Wallace's paper, he panicked. After twenty years of meticulous work, was he to be beaten at the final hurdle? On top of this, his 18-month-old baby son Charles died, filling him with grief.

Darwin's friends suggested that he write a summary of his main findings and publish it at the same time as Wallace. Darwin, as a senior and respected scientist, knew his paper would be given priority—and so it was. Later, Wallace and Darwin got to know each other well and enjoyed exchanging ideas. They continued to work in mutual support and friendship for many years, their respect for each other far outweighing any rivalry. Darwin even arranged financial support for Wallace when times got hard.

*On his travels, Wallace visited the island of Borneo in southeast Asia. While he was suffering from a fever on this island, with its rich animal and plant life, his ideas about the way species developed took shape. Like Darwin, Wallace was influenced by Malthus's writing about **populations.***

Wallace's ideas were not as carefully crafted as Darwin's, and were not backed up by years of research. However, his paper certainly forced Darwin to act. Astonishingly, both papers, published by the **Linnean Society,** went almost unnoticed. The society's president even complained that there had been no "striking discoveries" during the year! But once his ideas were public, Darwin raced ahead, determined to publish fully the theory he had worked on for so long.

A Book that Changed the World

Determined to write a book explaining his theory to everyone, Darwin began work during the family vacation on the Isle of Wight in July 1858. In spite of pain and illness, he kept going with furious intensity until the book was ready. In November 1859, *On the Origin of Species by Means of Natural Selection: or the Preservation of Favoured Races in the Struggle for Life*—quickly known as *The Origin of Species*—finally arrived in bookstores. Only 1,250 copies had been printed, and they sold out on the first day!

Hopes and fears

Long before he published his groundbreaking book, Darwin realized the trouble it would cause. In general, society accepted that all living organisms had been directly created by God in a single, original act of creation. However, more and more individuals had begun to question that view. In *The Origin of Species,* Darwin crystallized these thoughts and provided evidence to support them. In doing so, he fulfilled the hopes of his many supporters—but at the same time he fueled the worst fears of those who wanted no change in the way people viewed God and their position in society.

Few books have had greater impact—or caused more controversy—than The Origin of Species by Charles Darwin.

ON

THE ORIGIN OF SPECIES

BY MEANS OF NATURAL SELECTION,

OR THE

PRESERVATION OF FAVOURED RACES IN THE STRUGGLE
FOR LIFE.

BY CHARLES DARWIN, M.A.,

FELLOW OF THE ROYAL, GEOLOGICAL, LINNÆAN, ETC., SOCIETIES;
AUTHOR OF 'JOURNAL OF RESEARCHES DURING H. M. S. BEAGLE'S VOYAGE
ROUND THE WORLD.'

LONDON:
JOHN MURRAY, ALBEMARLE STREET.
1859.

The right of Translation is reserved.

Darwin used his work on barnacles and earthworms as part of the evidence for his ideas. This led to cartoons such as this one from Punch *magazine in 1882, which shows a worm "evolving" into a man, and finally into Darwin himself.*

MAN·IS·BVT·A·WORM·

The theory

The central idea of Darwin's book was that all living organisms have resulted from a long process of **natural selection.** Darwin was convinced that **reproduction** always produces more offspring than the environment can support. Those which are best adapted to their environment—the "fittest"—are the ones that will survive and breed themselves, passing on their successful characteristics. His theory was that all the **species** present on the earth were the result of this gradual process of **evolution,** of changing slowly over time, which he called "the survival of the fittest."

The book

Darwin crafted his book with haste but also great care, since he had spent so many years thinking about and working on his ideas. The first five chapters outline his theory. In the middle part of the book, he listed all the objections he expected people to raise against his ideas, and answered them. Finally, Darwin showed how many strange phenomena of the natural world can be explained by his theory of adaptive evolution.

The Great Debate

The publication of Darwin's book caused an uproar. Many people were hugely excited by the ideas he proposed and defended the whole principle of "Darwinism" with enthusiasm. Others resisted the thought that human beings, like all other living things, had **evolved** from more "primitive" ancestors. Meanwhile, Darwin avoided all the arguments and quietly retreated to his beloved Down House to carry on his work in private.

Darwin's dilemma

Although Darwin had no desire to rock the foundations of Victorian society, he was well aware of what he had done. It presented him with a dilemma. On the one hand, he wanted to debate and defend his ideas. On the other hand, he did not want to unsettle faithful Christians, and his health made constant debate and argument impossible. It was the Down House network of friends and colleagues, built up over the years, that saved the day. Many of his more vigorous friends fought the battles of evolution for him.

Thomas Henry Huxley was known as "Darwin's bulldog" because of his strong support for Darwin's ideas.

FELLOW SCIENTISTS

- Thomas Huxley and John Tyndall were strong supporters of Darwin, and well-known scientists in their own right. They were also both **atheists,** and one of their reasons for supporting Darwin so strongly was because they could use his ideas to deny the existence of God. Huxley's first comment on reading *The Origin of Species* was, "How extremely stupid not to have thought of that!"
- Alfred Russel Wallace and Joseph Hooker, eminent scientists who studied the links between biology and geography, were equally convinced by the scientific evidence Darwin presented. Unlike Huxley and Tyndall, they did not see any conflict between a belief in God and in the process of **natural selection,** believing that evolution was simply creation on a longer time scale.

Bishops and apes

In 1860, the **British Association for the Advancement of Science** arranged a debate at Oxford University on the subject of evolution. Huxley and Bishop Samuel Wilberforce were the main speakers. The discussion became very heated. When asked by the bishop whether he claimed to be descended from the apes on his grandfather's or his grandmother's side, Huxley replied that he would rather be descended from an ape than a man like the bishop!

The argument has never been entirely settled. The uproar over Darwin's book gradually died down, and now most scientists accept his theories, but many people feel they go against their religious beliefs.

The implication of Darwinism, that people were descended from apelike ancestors, gave cartoonists a field day! In this cartoon, published in 1859, an unknown artist drew Darwin showing an ape how alike the two of them were.

The barnacle books

Charles Darwin is remembered for his work on **evolution,** but that is only part of what he achieved. Darwin's inquiring mind led him into other famous and pioneering work. Darwin became interested in barnacles while at Edinburgh, and later he spent eight years intensively studying these tiny **crustaceans.** One of his children, visiting a neighbor and looking around the house, asked, "Then where does your father work on *his* barnacles?"— assuming that all fathers spent their time studying such creatures! Charles published two volumes on living barnacles and two on fossil forms that are still used in barnacle studies today.

A focus on plants

In the 1860s, while the battle stirred up by *The Origin of Species* was at its peak, Charles Darwin began a number of research projects with his son Francis. He used the lovely grounds of Down House for this work, so he had the opportunity to rest and listen to Emma reading whenever he felt tired or ill. He worked on the **pollination** of flowers, particularly orchids. His discoveries of the ways that flowers and their insect pollinators are so perfectly adapted to each other were more evidence for his theory of evolution.

A bee orchid is the perfect shape and size to receive a carpenter bee and coat it with pollen, and to receive pollen from other bees. Darwin had a new greenhouse built to help him grow the beautiful orchids he was studying with his son.

Charles and his son Francis then investigated the movements of plants, starting with how climbers twist their tendrils around supporting structures, and moving on to the idea that all plants are capable of movement.

They went on to do the first known work on plant *tropisms,* or movements in response to a particular stimulus. Together, father and son showed that the tip of a plant is sensitive to light from one direction, and that this influences growth lower down the shoot, so that the whole shoot bends towards the light. After additional work on **carnivorous plants,** they conducted a major study of earthworms and their role in keeping the soil fertile. Even if his work on evolution hadn't already made Darwin famous, any one of these findings would have!

ONGOING IMPACT   Into the future

Darwin's less well-known work on plant movements has influenced much of our modern knowledge of tropisms and plant **hormones.** In turn, this knowledge has led to the development of growth-control systems, ripening systems, and specialized weed killers, as well as the ability to **clone** plants from tiny fragments of the whole organism.

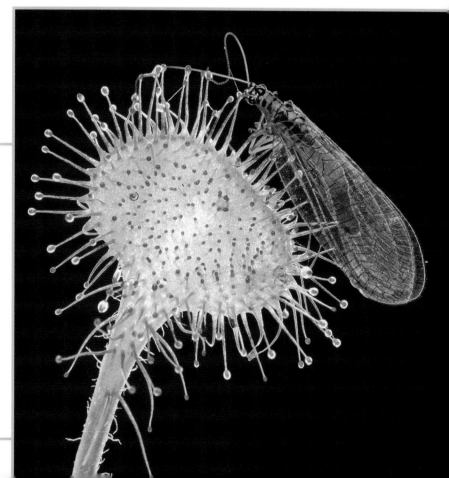

Darwin was fascinated by carnivorous plants, and was the first to realize that the ability to digest insects is an adaptation which allows plants to cope with very poor soil. This round-leaved sundew has caught a lacewing, which it will digest using special chemicals called enzymes, produced by the plant.

The Final Chapter

During the 1870s, Darwin's health improved. The stress of worrying about announcing his theory of **evolution** may have brought on much of his illness; now that things were out in the open, he was able to relax.

While he was still a young man, Darwin had lost his belief in a God who took a personal interest in the lives of people. In spite of the pleading and prayers of his wife Emma and his sisters, he never regained that faith. He did not follow his **atheist** friends, though, but remained **agnostic** to the end. He would never deny the existence of God, but he had serious doubts about the existence of an afterlife.

In old age, Darwin was an impressive figure, although his health was failing him by the time this picture was taken in 1881. He died the following year.

The death of Darwin

When Charles Darwin entered his seventies, his health went into a terminal decline. He felt constantly tired, walking wearied him completely, and he lost his enthusiasm and love of life. Early in 1882, he began to suffer from heart pains. One April night, he had a severe heart attack. When he regained consciousness, he said to his wife, "I am not in the least afraid to die." Despite Emma's constant care, he felt sick and faint for most of the day, and in the late afternoon of April 19, 1882, Charles Darwin—one of the greatest scientists the world has ever known—died at the age of 73.

In Darwin's words:

In 1879, Darwin wrote a letter describing his religious beliefs, in which he said: *"In my most extreme fluctuations I have never been an atheist in the sense of denying the existence of God. I think generally (and more and more as I get older), but not always, that an Agnostic would be the more correct description of my state of mind."*

The Darwin family assumed that Charles would be buried in the churchyard at Downe, along with the beloved children he had lost. However, many of his supporters wanted to have him buried with national honors. His wife and children, who had meant so much to him, agreed, so Charles Darwin was laid to rest in Westminster Abbey, along with many other great heroes from both science and the arts.

In spite of the controversy stirred up by Darwin's groundbreaking ideas, he was buried with honor beside other great scientists, such as Isaac Newton, Michael Faraday, and Charles Lyell, in Westminster Abbey.

Evolution in Action

After Darwin's death, his ideas declined somewhat in popularity. Without his presence to remind people of the real theory, and without his continual experiments in support of his ideas, Darwinism lost ground.

However, at the beginning of the twentieth century, the work of an Austrian monk named Gregor Mendel—which set out the **genetic** basis of inheritance of traits—became known and accepted. Although the men never met, Mendel's life and work overlapped with Darwin's, and their areas of study complemented each other perfectly. Darwin's ideas were now widely recognized as the only satisfactory explanation for the variety of life on Earth.

By the 1940s, studies in genetics, geology, statistics, and **population** biology had led to wider acceptance of Darwin's theory of **evolution.** Some fascinating examples of **natural selection** emerged, which showed clearly how the theory worked in practice. None of these studies would have been possible without Charles Darwin's pioneering work.

Gregor Mendel did many experiments with pea plants. When he died in 1884, Mendel was convinced that the world would soon acknowledge his discovery. How right he was!

GREGOR MENDEL

Gregor Johann Mendel (1822–1884) was the founder of the science of genetics, which would later help to explain Darwin's theory of evolution. Mendel was born to a poor Austrian family in 1822, and as a young man, he decided to become a monk. He worked away in isolation in his monastery at Brünn—now Brno in the Czech Republic—for many years, experimenting with crossing different strains of peas and carefully recording his findings. In 1866, Mendel presented his ideas on the breeding of peas, explaining their **dominant** and **recessive** traits—but his work was not accepted or understood in his own lifetime.

Peppered moths

In pre-industrial England, most specimens of *Biston betularia,* the peppered moth, were a speckled creamy color, with a few rare black forms. It was easy for predators to see the black ones against pale tree bark and eat them. But the **Industrial Revolution** caused smoke pollution, which turned many tree trunks dark, and suddenly it was the pale moths that were easy prey. The numbers of dark moths in the population increased until they were the more common color—they were "selected" when their color became an advantage. In recent years, the air has been cleaned up, the tree trunks are paler again, and the proportion of pale moths in the *Biston betularia* population is on the increase as natural selection takes its course.

Birds and butterflies

Some organisms have features which seem very similar—for example, birds, insects, and bats all have wings that allow them to fly. But these animals are not closely related, and their wings have developed, or evolved, quite separately.

Sometimes very similar structures are adapted for very different uses. A human hand, the flipper of a dolphin, and the leg of a horse have similar bones, which have been adapted for different functions. This is called *divergent evolution.*

Wings give a definite advantage, and many different animals, including these green-winged macaws, share this same selected trait. This is called convergent evolution.

Carrying the Torch

The ideas of Charles Darwin still affect many areas of biology. Much of our modern work on **genetics, social biology,** and conservation is supported by our understanding of the way **evolution** works on both a large and a small scale, as outlined by Darwin more than 150 years ago.

As we have developed an understanding of the way living organisms evolve by gradually adapting to their own environments, we have also become increasingly aware of the effect of a change in the environment on the organisms living there.

Adaptable oysters

In 1915, oyster fishermen in Malpeque Bay, Canada, noticed a few oysters with pus-filled blisters. By 1922, the oyster beds had been almost wiped out by a new and devastating disease. But a few shellfish contained disease-resistant genes. **Natural selection** meant these were the only oysters to survive and breed, so all the new oysters were resistant to disease as well. By 1940, oyster numbers were back to their old levels, and there was no disease.

Oyster yields from Malpeque Bay, Canada, changed over time. Only those oysters that had natural immunity to the new disease had offspring—survival of the fittest in action!

Saving the planet

On Earth today, environments are changing rapidly, and in very dramatic ways, as a result of human activity. Around the world, we pour out poisons from our factories and cars, we produce vast floods of sewage, and we destroy habitats. While living organisms have a built-in ability to adapt to change, if the change is too fast or too big, they cannot cope, and **species** are driven to the brink of extinction—and beyond.

The world has always changed, but today it is changing faster than ever. We must try to control the rate of this change if we are to save life on Earth as we know it. This area of rain forest in Indonesia is being cleared for timber, and the habitats of many rare animals are being destroyed with it.

God versus Darwin?

Although there is always discussion in the scientific community about the fine details of evolution, Darwin's basic principles are not in dispute among scientists. Still, not everyone agrees. For some people, there is no conflict between a deep faith in God and an acceptance of evolution. Others find this a problem. Religion is a system rooted in faith and unquestioned knowledge. It deals with spiritual things that cannot be explained simply by using scientific methods, which are based on collecting evidence and data in the natural universe.

The Great Theory

Charles Darwin was an outstanding character. As a young man, he spent five years traveling the world on the *Beagle*. In his personal relationships, Charles was ahead of his time—his relationship with his wife, Emma, was in many ways very modern. They were equal partners in many ways—sharing ideas, offering mutual support, and bringing up their children. Darwin adored his children, willingly leaving open his study door and allowing them to share in the excitement and interest of his discoveries.

The great scientist

During his lifetime, Darwin produced a great body of scientific work. His studies of barnacles and his pioneering work on plant movement have left their mark and are still relevant today. However, Darwin's greatest contribution by far to scientific understanding was his theory of **natural selection.**

Darwin was honored by scientists in his own time because his work made it possible for scientists and thinkers to study and discuss ideas which had always been denied before. Yet his theory has also stood the test of time. Modern scientists respect his original proposal of the mechanism for **evolution,** and it is still being refined and debated around the world today.

Darwin is a giant among giants—one of the great names of science, whose influence has lasted long after his death.

The work of Charles Darwin—shown here in 1842 with his oldest son—underpins almost every area of modern biology. He stands as one of the greatest scientists of all time.

A unifying theory

One of the great achievements of Darwin's theory of evolution by natural selection is that it has offered a unifying strand in biology, linking many different areas.

The great variety of life is a result of natural selection. **Genetic** variation creates organisms with a wide variety of characteristics, allowing selection to take place. Studying form and function shows just how well organisms can adapt to their environments. **Ecology** shows the adaptations of different organisms to each other. It also shows what happens when there are rapid changes to the environment—sometimes natural selection cannot provide adaptations to cope with these changes, and **species** become extinct.

Darwin's work has affected not only the science of biology, but also the structure of society itself. He raised the possibility of an alternative to divine creation, opening minds and sparking controversy at the same time. No matter what people think of Charles Darwin's theories, they will never forget his name.

Charles Darwin has earned his place in history by giving us a scientific explanation of just how the teeming variety of life arose, and how and why it continues to change.

Timeline

1798	Thomas Malthus publishes his *Essay on the Principle of Population.*
1809	Charles Robert Darwin is born in Shrewsbury, England, on February 12.
	Jean-Baptiste Lamarck publishes *Philosophie Zoologique,* in which he suggests that animals **evolve** to fit their environment, and that they pass on acquired characteristics to their offspring.
1817	Charles's mother, Susannah, dies.
1818	Charles goes to Shrewsbury School.
1825	Charles goes to Edinburgh University to study medicine. He starts to become an active **naturalist.**
1828	Charles goes to Cambridge University to study **divinity.** He meets Professor John Henslow and his interest in natural history grows.
1830–33	Charles Lyell publishes *Principles of Geology,* in which he suggests that the world may be hundreds of millions of years old.
1831	Charles Darwin joins the *Beagle* as naturalist and companion to Captain FitzRoy.
1832	The *Beagle* reaches Brazil in February. It spends three and a half years charting the waters of the South American coast. Darwin explores the **pampas** and discovers a number of new **species.**
1833	The British Parliament votes to **abolish** slavery throughout the British Empire.
1835	The *Beagle* reaches the Galápagos Islands. Darwin's attention is drawn to the variations between the **populations** of similar species on the different islands.
1836	The *Beagle* returns to England.
1837–38	Darwin places many of his specimens with other scientists and works in Cambridge on geology. He moves to London.
1837	Darwin becomes a member of the **Geological Society** and begins working with Charles Lyell.
1839	On January 29, Darwin marries his cousin Emma Wedgwood.
	He is granted Fellowship of the **Royal Society.**
	Emma Darwin gives birth to a son, William Erasmus.
	Darwin publishes *Journal of Researches into the Geology and Natural History of the Various Countries Visited by H.M.S. Beagle.*
1840	Darwin's health begins to deteriorate.
1841	Emma gives birth to a daughter, Anne.

1842	The Darwin family moves to Down House in Kent. Emma gives birth to a daughter, Mary Eleanor, who dies shortly after.
1851	Charles and Emma's daughter Anne dies.
1858	Darwin receives a paper from Alfred Russel Wallace, putting forward his own ideas about **natural selection.** Darwin and Wallace publish papers on natural selection with the **Linnean Society.**
1859	Darwin publishes *The Origin of Species*. It sells out on the first day.
1860	The **British Association for the Advancement of Science** holds a debate on evolution in Oxford. Thomas Huxley and Bishop Samuel Wilberforce lead the debate.
1860s	Darwin works with his son Francis on **pollination,** tropism, and earthworms.
1866	Gregor Mendel publishes his ideas on heredity.
1871	Darwin publishes *Descent of Man*.
1882	Charles Darwin dies at Down House on April 19, at the age of 73.

More Books to Read

Altman, Linda J. *Mr. Darwin's Voyage*. Parsippany, N.J.: Silver Burdett Press, 1995.

Parker, Steve. *Charles Darwin and Evolution*. Broomall, Penn.: Chelsea House Publishers, 1995.

Sunderland, Luther. *Darwin's Enigma—Ebbing the Tide of Naturalism*. Green Forest, Ark.: Master Books, 1998.

Glossary

abolition doing away with something

agnostic someone who does not know whether God exists and feels it is impossible to know

archipelago group of islands

atheist someone who does not believe in God

botany study of plants

British Association for the Advancement of Science association devoted to an increase in the public understanding of science. The association is still active today.

carnivorous plant plant that digests animals, usually insects, to provide itself with nutrients

classics Latin and Greek languages and history

clone animal or plant grown from the cells of another adult animal or plant and identical to its parent

crustacean animal in a class that includes crabs, lobsters, and shrimps, whose body has a hard outer shell

divinity study of God and religion

dominant type of gene that causes a trait to appear in an organism, whether it inherits one or two copies of the gene from the parents

ecology relationship between organisms and their environment, and between different species in an environment

economist someone who studies the way money is managed in society

evolution process by which species develop through natural selection

genetic engineering process of inserting a gene from one organism into the genetic material of another organism to change its characteristics

genetics study of the way characteristics are inherited

Geological Society society based in London dedicated to the study of geology

hormone chemical that carries messages around the body of an animal or plant

Industrial Revolution period of history when working practices and conditions were changed dramatically by the introduction of machines

invertebrate animal without a backbone

Linnean Society academic society, still in existence, named after Carolus Linnaeus, the man who developed the naming system for species of organisms

Lunar Society group of radical intellectuals who met monthly to discuss natural philosophy

marine living in the sea

naturalist person who studies natural objects such as plants and animals

natural selection process by which those individuals best fitted to survive in a particular environment are more likely to breed and pass on their desirable characteristics to their offspring

ornithologist person who studies birds scientifically

pampa large, grassy plain in South America

pollination transfer of pollen from the male part of the plant to the female part, often brought about by insects or the wind, depending on the type of plant

population group of organisms, all of the same species, living together in a particular habitat

public school in England, a private, fee-paying school

QED (quod erat demonstrandum) Latin for "that will be done"

radical in politics, a person who wants far-reaching change

recessive type of gene that can only cause a trait to appear in an organism if two copies of the gene are inherited, one from each parent

reproduction way in which animals and plants produce offspring

rhea large, flightless, ostrichlike bird found in South America

Royal Society most prestigious scientific society in Britain in Darwin's time and today

selective breeding process by which people choose animals with desirable traits for breeding, to produce offspring with the desirable characteristics—for example, breeds of dogs

social biology study of the social structures of animals

species group of closely related individuals that can breed together and produce fertile offspring

vicar clergyman in the Anglican church

Index